## A Visit to

# The Farm

by B. A. Hoena

**Consulting Editor:** Gail Saunders-Smith, Ph.D.

**Reading Consultant:** Jennifer Norford, Senior Consultant
Mid-continent Research for Education and Learning
Aurora, Colorado

Capstone
press

Mankato, Minnesota

Pebble Plus is published by Capstone Press
151 Good Counsel Drive, P.O. Box 669, Mankato, Minnesota 56002
www.capstonepress.com

1  2  3  4  5  6  09  08  07  06  05  04

*Library of Congress Cataloging-in-Publication Data*
Hoena, B. A.
The farm/by B. A. Hoena.
p. cm.—(Pebble plus, A visit to)
Includes bibliographical references and index.
Contents: The farm—Farm buildings—Farm animals—Fields and crops.
ISBN 0-7368-2390-5 (hardcover)
1. Farms—Juvenile literature. 2. Agriculture—Juvenile literature. [1. Farms. 2. Agriculture.] I. Title.
II. Series.
S519.H57 2004
630—dc22                                                          2003011991

**Editorial Credits**
Sarah L. Schuette, editor; Jennifer Bergstrom, series designer; Kelly Garvin, photo researcher;
    Karen Risch, product planning editor

**Photo Credits**
Bruce Coleman Inc./IFA-Animals, 11
Capstone Press/Gary Sundermeyer, front cover (cow), 1, 4–5, 8–9, 12–13, 15, 16–17, 18–19, 20–21
Corbis, front cover (crops); Macduff Everton, 7
Digital Vision, front cover (barn)
PhotoDisc Inc., back cover (pig)

Pebble Plus thanks the Minnesota Agricultural Interpretive Center, Waseca, Minnesota, for the use of its farm
for photo shoots.

## Note to Parents and Teachers

The series A Visit to supports national social studies standards related to the production,
distribution, and consumption of goods and services. This book describes and illustrates
a visit to a farm. The images support early readers in understanding the text. The
repetition of words and phrases helps early readers learn new words. This book also
introduces early readers to subject-specific vocabulary words, which are defined in the
Glossary section. Early readers may need assistance to read some words and to use
the Table of Contents, Glossary, Read More, Internet Sites, and Index/Word List sections
of the book.

**Word Count: 113**
**Early-Intervention Level: 14**

# Table of Contents

# The Farm

A farm is a fun place
to visit. Farms have buildings,
fields, and animals.

# Farm Buildings

Barns are large buildings where animals live. Barns also hold crops and equipment. Farmers milk cows in barns.

Bins hold food that

farm animals eat.

Bins are round and wide.

# Farm Animals

Chickens look for food
around the farm.
They peck at the ground.

Sheep graze. They eat
the grass in a pasture.

Pigs stay in their pens.

Pigs snort and squeal.

# Fields and Crops

Farmers use tractors
in their fields. Tractors
pull heavy machinery.

Farmers drive combines.
Combines help farmers pick
or harvest crops in the fall.

A farm is an important place. The food people and animals eat comes from a farm.

# Glossary

barn—a building where animals, crops, and equipment are kept

combine—a powerful vehicle that picks or harvests crops when they are finished growing in a field

field—an area of land used for growing crops

graze—to eat grass that is growing in a field or pasture

pasture—the land that animals use to graze

tractor—a powerful vehicle that has large wheels; tractors pull farm machinery, hay wagons, and heavy loads.

# Read More

**Schuh, Mari C.** *Cows on the Farm.* On the Farm. Mankato, Minn.: Pebble Books, 2002.

**Stanley, Mandy.** *On the Farm.* New York: Kingfisher, 2002.

**Weber, Rebecca.** *Foods from the Farm.* Spyglass Books. Minneapolis: Compass Point Books, 2004.

# Internet Sites

FactHound offers a safe, fun way to find Internet sites related to this book. All of the sites on FactHound have been researched by our staff.

Here's how:

1. Visit *www.facthound.com*

2. Type in this special code **0736823905** for age-appropriate sites. Or enter a search word related to this book for a more general search.

3. Click on the Fetch It button.

FactHound will fetch the best sites for you!

# Index/Word List